The Nameless

poems by

Jed Myers

Finishing Line Press
Georgetown, Kentucky

The Nameless

ACKNOWLEDGMENTS

I am grateful to the editors of the journals noted below for their earlier publication of the
poems here listed:

"Life Story" first appeared in *Bacopa Literary Review*.
"Squirrel Cove" first appeared in *Windfall*.
"Still in His Chest" first appeared in *Sanskrit*.
"Loyal" first appeared in *Euphony*, and later in *Floating Bridge Review*.
"Union Square" first appeared in *The MacGuffin*.
"He Laughed" first appeared in *Fault Lines*.
"Half to Blame" first appeared in *Pedestal*, and later in *Studio One*.
"Exhibition" and "The Elsewhere Inside You" first appeared in *The Monarch Review*.
"His Last Season" first appeared in *The Journal of the American Medical Association*.
 Copyright © (2011) American Medical Association. All rights reserved.
"Up from LA" first appeared in *Moon City Review*.
"The Lip of Emptiness" first appeared in *Floating Bridge Review*.
"Million Dollar Pier" first appeared in *Barely South Review*.

My thanks goes to many, more than I can possibly name in this space, who have supported
me in the writing and gathering of these poems. The keen and caring eyes of fellow poets
T. Clear, Jim Bertolino, Kathleen Flenniken, Lana Ayers, Ted McMahon, Peter Munro, and
C. Albert have been essential to the alchemy of this collection's creation. Ashley Brumett
has been deeply encouraging of my immersion in the mysterious process by which this
work has come into being. Leah Maines of Finishing Line Press has envisioned these
poems lasting, and Christen Kincaid (also of FLP) has worked diligently to fulfill this
vision. Rosanne Olson has graciously provided the cover imagery that is now the window
into the book. To these lovely souls, and to many others, I am endlessly grateful.

Editor: Christen Kincaid
Cover Art: Rosanne Olson
Author Photo: Rosanne Olson
Cover Design: Elizabeth Maines

Table of Contents

—to all who in passing reveal
something of our nature

The Nameless

We meet them in silence by daylight
and daydream their histories. How
did the fast-walking man in shorts come to list
to his right? He passes each afternoon
with never an instant of eye-contact.
What is he limping away from?

We meet without a nod in the mix
of moonlight and streetlamp. Where
does that woman, thick-rimmed and long-coated, go
when she gets off the bus? Does she enter
a dark apartment? She said hello
to someone once, with a southern accent.

We see them through two shatterproof panes
in the next lane, at the long red light
we are agreed to obey, and wonder
does she, or he, also wish
for just the kind of touch we've missed
since that bewildering day....

No point naming them. They will not be
illuminated by such facts—they're shadowed
enough by all the answers they offer
themselves. The nameless—let them be
so. How bright they are in the ever-
sudden light of a moment's wonder.

Walking at Night

Night's flowers are their own shadows.
They wear the silk of light's absence.

Depending on the moon or the clouds
where you are, such blooms can be visible.

Depending also on the invisible
churn of events inside you, you might notice

the irises outside a house
rising from the earth of a bed

where someone, years back, had nested
the rootstock. Someone had turned

and sifted the earth in this place—you might've
witnessed this on a morning walk,

and thought, Sometimes we bend
to our wishes, even wishes that wait

to bloom through us at night as we turn,
shoulder to shoulder, between dreams.

Someone steps out in the new light,
then into the shadows of the ramshackle

shed, spiders and all, to reach
through webs for the trowel, to begin again

making a wish rise from the soil,
while another someone still sleeps.

The wish itself will remain invisible.
What grows out of it will be something

else—wind-jostled, dressed
in cloud-shred, moon-silver, moonlessness...

like the spread of shivering iris
petals you pass walking at night.

You can guess what radiance held
in someone's vision, before first light.

On My Way to the Dentist

The dead are walking in our midst,
crossing the marble floor of the lobby.
They too are here on business.

And on the elevator in their black
silk pajamas, mingling with us
chest-to-chest in silence. Look, one
just inside the sliding metal
door as it seals shut, a hint
of IV tubing hanging from her
thin translucent wrist—she's pressed
up against the man who sold her
long-term care insurance. There,

another, singed holes in his tunic,
squeezed into the corner (just like flesh),
head turned from the smoker's breath
of the stout smartly-dressed Republican
just back from a deal in Pakistan.
The dead man can't tell
what part that fellow played in his death—
the dead are not telepathic.
It just works out like this.

There are so many, now that we notice!
More of them than us.
Altogether, exceeding the limit
on the permit over the panel of buttons.
Still, the lift lifts.

Walking out with me on my way
to the dentist, my mother's first husband,
pale as hell since that battle in Italy.

Life Story

Say, the nameless nonexistence said,
Why not a universe! So stars appeared,

and these—no one watching how they bled
in lonely rage their white plasmic radiance

across the empty reaches of the night,
no hope to kiss the sand of singing beaches

that had not been invented yet—these useless
suns burned on for no one, till they noticed

small forms forming, rounded spinning magnets,
clustered dust. The planets had begun

their faithful orbits, silent and adoring,
or hungry, or indifferent, varied much

like children. Some clung so close they burned
away their clothes and melted off their faces.

Some were stoic, stayed remote, and froze.
These looked the other way. These hurt the most.

In middle distances, some planets bathed
their skins in air and water. So begins

the chapter in which life concocts itself.
Molecular traditions mark the seasons.

The senses bloom among the moving creatures,
soon so complex, we'll call it consciousness.

And gathered round a fire in some brush land
on one such middling planet or another,

a mammal child with a fiery tongue
unclasps the nipple to invent the word

that troupe will say for love without her knowing
what bright dust they were and will become.

She falls back on the breast to watch the stars.

Twelve

The old man's lover has little pale nipples
on spare flesh—no matter. Though she's much
younger, she's his secret mother. She startles

at night, her brother's flesh wild inside her
again—the old man's quiet penetration
a comfort. Girl whose teeth decayed

for the loss of her mother at twelve, she shaves
the coarse hairs of her groin and legs
to be the child she was. She drinks

five beers at the dive bar before she rings
his apartment at twelve. She's his secret
mother in her bare protuberant ribcage.

Squirrel Cove

Scraps of lives lay among the stones
and shells above the tideline—shattered

cups and saucers, a rusted wrench,
plastic bottles far from the mouths

their mouths touched, tattered shirts
and jackets tucked amid bleached logs,

oarlocks, knotted stretches of nylon
line, shredded netting, dull black

latex of a treadless tire perhaps once
hung from a gunwale. We said nothing

as we passed, our steps grinding
the shells into the stones—the music

to which we imagined these things being
set loose from lives like our own.

Before They Could Know

There's a woman whose synapses extend
out to her backyard's apple branches,

and beyond, through her part of town's
neglected orchards, farther, through the woods

down by the lake and around in that tangle
that reaches as far as the forests

rising into the clouds, her mind
spread wide in this vast antenna array,

so she knows, without knowing
how or why, a car's coming

along the highway under the half-moon,
a man driving to the city to find her,

though they've only met a few times
as presences in the treetops, and it seemed

it was just the backs of their minds, opened
with long-ago climbs to familiar boughs

near their houses, across the mountains
from each other, before they could know

what it is to call out across space and time
through the mind of the world to your lover.

Still in His Chest

A young warrior wanders the airport
in his fresh-laundered chaos-cloth
colored sage, eucalyptus, tumbleweed.

Guess he's had to murder a fair lot
of boys his own age, no Goliath
but terrified men who stumble and bleed.

Still he's beefed-up on belief, hair short
as Astroturf, eyelids like fast moth
wings. Doesn't know what he'll need

for relief back here—might be weed,
Oxycontin, beer, white froth
of speed in a spoon…. He's just bought

a little golden bear for his kid—
holding it seems to quiver his mouth.
He grits his teeth, temples taut

as tripwire. Who knows what he did
over there. Has his soul flown south?
I bet it's still in his chest, in a knot.

Loyal

Stacks of bills on the marble
dining room table, unopened cards
and letters (*sympathy* and still
some *get well*) scattered over
the kitchen counter, lists
on lined paper of accounts
where funds are held tucked under
long term care brochures
and prescription pill bottles,
the upstairs closets filled
with garments of no use here now,
cards with attorneys' numbers
on both bedroom dressers,
the nightstands' and the bathroom
drawers stuffed with the reminders
of obsolete necessities, slips
of colored memo pads still sticking
everywhere, and all the pictures,
books, clocks, boxes, curios…
the furniture of course, rugs
and tapestries, the curtains
shading no one from the glare
of the world, the house itself,
the ground it sits on still
requiring care—it comes down
to hair gel tubes, paperclips, scissors,
the little bronze French officer
under which lies the grocery list,
the almost-empty jar of marmalade
on the bottom shelf in the fridge,
and the dozens of frozen foil-wrapped
restaurant leftovers that would wait
forever if we let them. Things can be
loyal, more loyal than we are,
holding still, even for the dead.

Union Square

In the late day shadows of Macy's, Victoria's
Secret, the Hilton, the St. Francis
and the Sir Francis Drake Hotels,

they held out their hands and cups, nails
untrimmed and edged with the dark of dirt
that rubbed the shadow into their skins.

And each was a certain person—one toothless
and yellow-eyed, almost shouting, one showing
his amber teeth with a smile of greeting, one

shaking (for lack of drink, dread, untreated
Parkinson's?), one with red lightning streaks
emanating from the pewter of cataracts

clouding her pupils. How was I seen
in the mind of one pauper close to the corner
and seated back to a trashcan, the wind

reaching down under her purple sweatshirt
and my silk-and-wool scarf to steal
what heat it could from our hides, each of us

dealing with the one impatient tide,
the crowd swelling and dense at the light,
we both in the jostle of human urgency,

I in my hurry to find a good place
for a bite before my ride to the airport,
she in her stalwart polite beseeching,

frayed mouth of a Starbuck's cup calling
out from the weave of grit-blackened fingers—
how did she see me? Source of the buck

I stuffed on top of the few dimes and quarters
in her cup? Pitying jerk with a conscience
disease this was a weak way to treat?

A blur of luck? I don't know
if I even brought myself to look at her
soul to soul for an instant at least.

I steered my flesh through the shifting
gaps in the chaos and crossed the street,
still half-convinced it was will, not wealth,

that lifted me on toward that meal, my flight,
my city and bed before midnight—not
the star-wind roaring in all our births.

He Laughed

He was last seen on the Bremerton ferry.
A late-summer weekday morning.
He'd stopped at the gas station, stopped
at the ATM (had punched the code—
was compos mentis). He might have believed
he was headed for the office. Did he seem
on edge on the deck? He didn't flinch
at the horn-blast. We know he lingered
to watch the wake from the rail, aft.
And the gulls—his eyes lifted up
to take them in as they followed the craft
out onto the cold expanse. We believe
he laughed along with them for a moment.
This is when he was last seen.

Half to Blame

There's the little rumpled half-man
who lives above the bar. He eats
falafel without the pita, drinks
half-pints of beer, smokes
half a cigarette here
and there—half-kisses
half-hearted women who half-
listen to his poems when they're half-
written. He drives
a half-dead car. He's lived past
the invisible halfway mark
of life. Half the time he wishes
he had a wife. But he's half-
certain she would drive him half-
insane. She'd wind up taking half
of everything, and he'd be half
to blame. The little man has half
a mind to wander half a world
away. Who would miss him, half
his friends and family dead already,
the rest half-interested? He's half-
glad to be this free. Up half
the night, half-convinced he's lonely,
he can't see why he should be.
Little crumpled half-man, half
the man he could be, half-blind
with half-baked rage behind
the half-lies of his conscious mind,
he knows he doesn't know
the half of it, and having half
the truth might be a kindness.

Exhibition

She, the body artist, devoted her flesh
to the stark portrayal of what we'll do for love.
The stage and blade were set. She'd carve one fresh
long wound in her pale skin, say, thigh, above
the knee's taut hide, then lie on her side, her head
at rest on a propped palm. The gash would first
appear linear, unreal, penned, then widen red
and sprout a rivulet at one end. We'd thirst
for glimpses into the emptiness, but it was full,
a crimson canal of bright sacrifice. She'd place
the knife down neatly, thread the needle, and pull
black twine through twin pierced edges, with no trace
of pain—no wince, nor flinch—she'd stitch herself tight,
slow, serene, then rise and walk out in the night.

His Last Season

Still courting lymphoma, intending
to flirt again tonight with a dozen
exotic neoplasms, bones cooked
for years to a brittle foam in smoke
and ethanol, he leads with his big-liver
pre-diabetic belly and tangos
out the door after dinner, heart
harassed to an adequate squeeze where it sags
on his heaving diaphragm. He wheezes
toward the car to cart himself
downtown once more to *Ibiza*
for the evening Flamenco show. He knows
he's riding on hopes worn past all traction,
bald as the radials barely holding
his Buick to the rain-slicked road. He skids
like a hepped-up kid when he pulls in, pops
a cigarette between his lips for the half-
a-city-block walk to the door, and once
inside, he's looking—
                              Love,
still hiding, might blow in tonight
through a portal in the music and uplift him
on the cadences of the talk with a woman
he's about to meet. Love could pour
through the alley between the crumpled towers
of his lungs, stir high all at once
the tossed-out scores, loose papers,
the unsigned, unfinished stories
of his lost days, rediscovered,
alive even now in this his last season,
not because he's earned Love's gift
with any courage or devotion,
nor has his suffering deserved it, but
the muse (Some evenings, she observes
the dancers from the tall gold curtains…)—
she could return, to return the uncertain

kiss he left, the night of his first
whiskey, on the lips of the girl
he never saw before or since,
to welcome him at last to his own
disappearance, to dance with him once
while his stretched spirit still sticks
to his guts, or for no human reason.

Up from LA

The local madman seems to know
he's on the air. As we round the corner
he offers his listeners a review
of the local universe—we two,

producer and young star, he's sure,
arm in arm down the street to the car;
we'll cruise to the seaside hotel
to rehearse, in bed, our new thriller,

while our commentator finds an alcove
for himself and his cart of shreds,
covers himself with his coat,
wraps the night up with his guests....

Psychosis—so sure of itself,
distilling its own cure of the dreads
with which it floods the senses. His
voice is definite—he *knows*

we're up from LA, on one of those
junkets of mutual self-display,
dressing and undressing together
as if the cosmos were our little theater,

all terrors at bay. On the street
where he sleeps, the gray asphalt
membrane bounces his announcements
into space, that treble sharpness

reflecting the hardness of the world.
How many listeners are out there?
I can imagine an immense audience.
He broadcasts bursts of certainty

out into a populous nowhere, facts—
the armies of Narcissus on Earth
in the Age of Mirrors, strolling in pairs
and catching their images in the glass.

The Lip of Emptiness

He chalks and chalks the cue,
sets down the little cube,
its blue crater upward
toward the stars, then crouches

for the shot, and waits—
how he's made the last few.
Slow. His young opponent's fast.
They're years apart. Well-matched.

He told me, not an hour ago,
as he slid his emptied pint
into the windowsill's red neon
light, still, he didn't know

how they found her—the wife
he'd left. She never answered that
last call. Confessed he'd kept on
loving her. Did she do it?

His eyes fix on a nonexistent
string of impacts—blue tip
to strike the ivory sphere to hit
the bright-striped 9 to cross

the green field and kiss the lip
of emptiness. The adversary
taps a foot, but that's not it.
The old fellow's intentness slips—

an image, a human object,
drops in through the pupil aimed
across the felt. It's this,
the witness, taking in the game.

Million Dollar Pier

Skin hot, sore, itching from the day
under August sun on the beach in just trunks,
I'd cherish the night's breeze washing over
my face and what cool air seeped under
my madras shirt and corduroy jeans,
out in the toasty creosote stink
laced with whiffs of roasting peanuts,
sizzling dogs, those infinite pink
and blue strands of cotton candy in skeins
bigger than kids' heads, cigarette plumes,
ten-cent cigar fumes, all these
threads embroidering the raw silk
of the surf's wet-rot scent spread over us
(evidence of the saltwater crests
tossing themselves against the world
in the darkness yards under our feet
and shredding the seaweed, crushing shells,
macerating the carapaces of sand crabs
decimated in the tumble we heard
without listening), the churn stirring
and lifting the mist of invisible droplets,
lending a subliminal shine
to everything visible. We never see
why we are anywhere at the time.
Amid the smells in that festival
racket of roller coasters, start-up bells,
the repetitive jarring jingles
of eternal childhood emanating
from the big-kid and kiddie carousels, came
etheric wafts of the girls' perfumes,
purchased or shoplifted in Woolworth's
or off mom-&-pop corner drugstore aisles
(the evidence, in volatile traces,
available in the happenstance weave
through the human clusters heaving
from funhouse exit to Ferris wheel,
skee ball concession to rifle row's
incessant procession of metal ducks)—

the scents caught anywhere, sudden, unsought,
off the bare necks of the girls I would never
know better—the why in the why
I was there with Marty, Richie, and Bobby,
abandoning drums, keyboard, guitars,
forgetting TV or any real dinner
and stalking the boardwalk's fast mile
from Richie's house to this rinky-dink magic
peninsula, Million Dollar Pier,
seeking, secretly from myself,
the evidence (in the glare of the million
dumb-colored bulbs strung through the struts
of this rickety storm-taunting monstrosity)
of desire, borne in the form
of that other I desired mystified
and afraid, and afraid it would show
in those goddesses' eyes. They were made-up
to excess, masked in opaque pancake
and demonesque eye-shadow, eyebrows dark
as the night out over the sea, skirted
or slacked in mysteriously elastic cloth,
and bloused in poor boy sweaters so loose
I could see through the weave's little windows
the flesh upheld in the snug synthetic
baskets of their bras. I could read
the row-house dignity in their whispers
into each other's big-hooped ears,
and admire their aversion of gaze
from me, their eyes cartooned with liner
to say they are waiting for someone in leather
or tall and bold enough to stand there
before one of them and offer
a smoke, a stick of gum, some calm
company on that ride that flies out
through the dark, a try at the satiny
stuffed prize for toppling the pins
with one true pitch, something

in the code of cool that was called-for
of which I hadn't a clue. I didn't
want to sleep with one of these sweet-scented
bearers of evidence of such desire—
I only wished to someday have slept
with someone like this, one of these still-distant
emissaries of a land out of reach,
across a sea I could not yet imagine
myself across, however near,
nearer than ever when I wove
with my friends through the glitz among girls
who skirted the night giving off hints
of what might be possible elsewhere.

If He Does Not

He notices she's noticing him—
he thinks, before thought, she's tipsy
on hope or desire set afloat

as of her last mishap—look,
that furrow of doubt, a line out
the corner of her left eye. That's all

he needs to see. He's crossed
in and out of these madnesses—they're like islands,
each with its sorcery, its delusions

and masks, its cocktails and dances,
its favorite bars. In this one
reverie, we don't know what she sees

in him—in her trance, he might be
the uncle who touched her there, disguised
for now in fresh anonymity, still

desirable for the night—is it he
whose arousal will prove so pure,
a blood with no will to clot,

such that when he is pushed away,
he's the wounded child, and her mercy
the only tourniquet? So far

in this eternity, no one can say.
If he does not avert his own eyes
and leave the bar, in his mind

satisfied it's better he's lashed
to the mast against beauty and all
its regrets, he might discover it.

We want him leaning toward her,
watching the crease to the side of her eye
disappear, for now, whatever

truth proves itself to the squinting
observer by the brightness of day,
tomorrow, next summer, next year....

Afternoon Rain

A man stands in a winter rain.
He stands there and makes something of it.

He takes the sky as a great gray newspaper
open to the day's events, vast pages

filling in anyone who wants to know,
simply by gravity and a little wind—

its cold sizzle of senselessness chills
his skin, his bones. He wants to know.

Most of the news is how well we've done
in the weapons business—with guns

and other instruments, where it rains
and never rains, from fists to rockets

and high-energy beams, grenades
and ropes binding wrists, with choppers

and horses, drones and torches,
flags, oaths, and prayers twisting

young men's musculature and lust
into private and tribal rapes.

The clouds catch him up on facebook
humiliations, gang initiations

by the hurdle of murder, torture
training in certain unspecified centers,

Bond and Batman and Hulk flicks pumping
purposeless sons up into fantasy

soldiers and real soldiers. The rain is
informative—its multitudinous impacts,

the heavens' news, a complex music.
A spectrum of notes from thud to ping,

it rumbles, rings, mutters....
It's a military transport's roar

diffused and muffled by the city's noise,
the sputter of worked-up boys

in a chaotic classroom. The staccato
of single-shooter hits in a video

game that snares the otherwise impaired
attention of a smart scared scary kid,

the soft *thwip* of a dart's tip entering
the disc of cork on a pub's paneled wall,

the mass rasp of thousands in the tiers
at the Sunday mass of American football,

the auditory jumble under the helmet
that's hardly cushioned the *n*th concussion

on the fall on the run toward the goal,
all the armored warriors slipping

in the mud, and he hears it well.
He reads the report of the clouds,

listening to the world's-end whimper
in the hum of an overhang gutter. He's wet

with the pure invisible helplessness we are
all meant to discover is real,

real in the heart of the weird kid's mother,
in the bound wrists of a naked soldier,

in the hands of the boy who can't hold
his terror in the cage of his chest any more,

real in the shivering core of the man
standing in the afternoon rain

that is only water falling from the sky.
The shining water we thrive by.

Diner Stop

She's not totally tattooed, but
florid scenes of her sojourns
in Guatemala and Belize
cover the curved plains of her arms
and shoulders. How many hours
has she held still for the outlines
and bold colorings of those ferns,
trumpeting blossoms, upright birds
whose beaks like golden swords divide
lush mountainsides…?

                     I stir
the coffee she's brought me, long
past the moment the sugar dissolves,
watching the tropics recede as she walks
toward the kitchen—she'll see
if my side of fresh fruit is ready.

I discern a cold wind in the trees
losing their leaves—I don't get why
the wide windowpane doesn't fog inside
with steam from the undulant jungle
under her skin. The glass transmits
the gleam of the late-November day.

Her half-bare shoulders have me wondering
where the banana and cantaloupe come from
anyway. Somewhere near the equator?

She'll serve me without knowing,
leaning over to set the bowl down
before me, revealing the monkey
luxuriating under the palms
in the little valley just over the ridge
of her left clavicle. She'll tell me
again how Nicaragua will fit
in that expanse down past
the crest of one of her hips.

I'll chew my fruit chunks, sip
my coffee, and imagine some trips.

The Elsewhere inside You

You, thin woman from a sunburned country,
who cut and color your hair like straw
so you look like a wind-blown boy off a field;

you, who sit in the bar down the block
a few nights a week when your husband's gone off
on another deal; you, fast-hearted

large-eyed long-limbed thirster for talk,
who grabbed me to dance with you once in that dive
for a minute, easy to lead; you,

bendable orphan, who laugh through your teeth
at the ungainly grace of your own wrists and fingers
kneading the air whose motes are the yeast

of your outlander speech; you, who can't help
but dare, by your willowy lean on the man
tending his beer beside you, to seem

familiar, as if he'd known you for years—
now that it's late, and clear, and the stars are out
over our neighbor apartment towers,

and I've stepped out on my deck to abide
the unknowable distances, there you are
by yourself on the sidewalk not far from your door,

collar up on that gangly-elegant neck,
exhaling a little white plume of your death,
the orange spot at the end of your cigarette

dimming in the cold air. I imagine
your tongue, salty and desperate, darting
in and out of another man's mouth

not an hour earlier back in that shack
just after last call, and I think
that you want to be known more than you know—

that the elsewhere inside you, like a hare
who forages on your memory's stubble,
won't let your heart slow. Sleep must be trouble.

At the Airport

Waiting on the Arrivals level
   where the escalator delivers up
its boluses of travelers after
   their subway ride from the International
Concourse, I watched a woman
   with short hair pace but keep her eye
on the appearing faces. After
   maybe half an hour, a man
stepped off the rising stairway and ran
   in that woman's direction, while she
held her hands to the sides of her head
   till he stood before her. Then
they embraced. They held each other
   on and on, close as two
clothed persons in a public space
   could get. Barely moving,
they remained this way, while I,
   still waiting for my arriving
company, had plenty of time
   to imagine these lovers' lives,
their long separation (was it for war
   or money, or important studies?),
and how, now, with their bodies,
   they promised each other more
eternity than either could ever
   deliver, but were, in that silent
utterly mutual oath, telling
   one another the truth.

J ed **Myers** is a Philadelphian living in Seattle, where he is a psychiatrist with a therapy practice. His book-length collection, *Watching the Perseids*, received the 2013 Sacramento Poetry Center Book Award. He won the 2012 Mary C. Mohr Editors' Award offered by *Southern Indiana Review*, received the 2013 *Literal Latte* Poetry Award, and was a 2013 Puchcart Prize nominee. His poems have appeared in *Prairie Schooner*, *Nimrod International Journal*, *Crab Orchard Review*, *Barely South Review*, *Atlanta Review*, *Heron Tree*, *Grey Sparrow Journal*, *Crab Creek Review*, *The Journal of the American Medical Association*, and elsewhere.